Dedication

This book is dedicated to the **Elite Ones**...the never-stop-'til-they're-at-the-top educators who are not one ounce like people who "just teach."

We don't identify with the status quo, other educators who are phoning it in, blaming others and counting down the days to retirement.

In fact, we are a rare breed who have answered the teaching call and refuse to accept anything less than full responsibility for the performance of our students and our schools.

We are education radicals who aren't afraid of high standards, expectations and accountability...in fact, we welcome it.

If you ask the typical educator, they'll tell you that we need to get real about our expectations and stop dreaming. But the truth is, every day we see formerly failing students and schools rising up and changing their trajectory.

Just like that.

And, it's happening through first class skill, first class professionalism and first class heart.

We are the Elite Ones, and this is what we do.

Does this describe you? If so, message me at jill@jackson-consulting.com and tell me "I am an **Elite One**!"

I would love to hear from you!

Jill Jackson

CONTENTS

THE SIMPLIFIED

LESSON PLANNING
FORMULA

A Whole New Take on Lesson Planning
That Helps You Build Lessons You'll
Actually Teach

BY

Jill Jackson

OTHER BOOKS WRITTEN
BY JILL JACKSON

Get a Backbone, Principal!

Get Some Guts, Coach!

How to Teach Students to Critically Think About Text

How to Teach Students to Write Informational Text

How to Coach Teachers to Teach Almost Anything

All titles available at jackson-consulting.com

In order for us to feel completely **CONFIDENT** in our ability to plan and deliver a killer lesson, we have to dump some old practices that don't net us much and replace them with some **BRAND-NEW** thinking and practices.

The Simplified Lesson Planning Formula

SCRATCHING MY OWN ITCH

Every book I have written (this is my 6th!) came from desperately needing simple teaching solutions and not being able to find them!

It all started back at the University of Redlands when I was in my education classes. I was a born teacher and there I was: learning the ins and outs of what real teachers did! I was beyond excited.

I remember being in one class and spending a week on a 14-step lesson plan (I'm not kidding) and feeling soooo accomplished because I had this beautiful Bloom's Taxonomy-driven lesson plan that was ready to be taught to 5th graders!

What didn't dawn on me (until I showed that lesson plan to my master teacher), was that the 10-page lesson plan that took me a week to write was for ONE SUBJECT...taught in ONE LESSON...in ONE HOUR. I mean, if I was going to have to lesson plan like this for 5 or 6 subjects every single day, I would never have a life!

That's when I realized that there was a gap between what I was being taught in college and what I needed for real-life teaching, but I didn't know how to fix it. Once I left college, people just assumed I knew how to lesson plan.

So, I would take my lesson plan book with its tiny boxes and jot down the number of the lesson I would teach (ex: Unit 6, Lesson 17), the page numbers in the teacher's guide (ex: Unit 6, pg. 123-141) and the materials that I would need to prep (ex: writer's notebook, highlighters, alternate text #3

and graphic organizer #2). It still didn't feel like I had done anything other than create a to-do list for myself, but at least it was more realistic than that 14-step lesson plan template!

And then, to confuse things even more, at one point I was handed a scripted curriculum. Essentially, the work had been done for me because it told me what to teach and how to teach it. I couldn't help but wonder exactly what I was supposed to do with my lesson plan book if it had already been done. I was honestly confused.

I began to see lesson planning as a hoop to be jumped through...something to be turned in to my principal each week. It wasn't what I needed it to be: a tool to make me an excellent teacher who regularly brought all my students to mastery.

So, I created this formula to scratch my own itch and solve my own lesson planning dilemma. I wanted to finally feel confident and in control of my lessons. And I've learned that lessons are made or broken in the lesson planning stage.

I hope this book helps you feel like I now do: confident in your ability to take a standard, goal or outcome and put together a lesson that is highly focused and leads each of your students to mastery.

In order for us to feel completely confident in our ability to plan and deliver a killer lesson, we have to dump some old practices that don't net us much and replace them with some brand-new thinking and practices.

This book is your roadmap for keeping what's important and replacing the rest with only what will serve your teaching and your students best.

WHAT IS THE SIMPLIFIED LESSON PLANNING FORMULA?

The Simplified Lesson Planning Formula is a series of steps that you will take to lesson plan for every school year, every subject and every class.

A formula is a fixed series of steps designed to get a specific result. The Simplified Lesson Planning Formula is a three-step method that will allow you to standardize your lesson planning. This intentional method will help you get consistent results with your students regardless of what or who you are teaching!

Here are the easy-to-implement steps you'll learn:

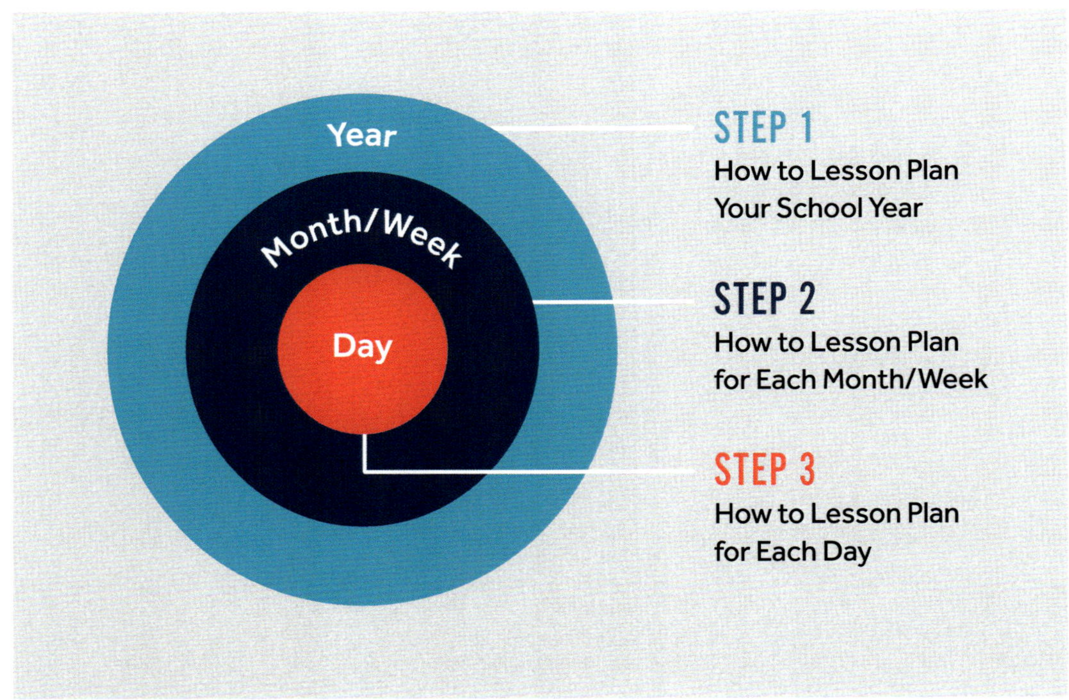

SKILL DRIVEN *vs.* CONTENT DRIVEN LESSON PLANNING

Unfortunately, lesson planning has become hyper-focused on "teaching the content" or "making it through the unit/chapter/semester."

I am going to ask you to think completely differently.

You are going to hear me reference "skill" again and again throughout this book.

The reason why I use the term "skill" instead of just "content" is because a skill is an ability which, once mastered, can be taken by students from subject to subject and school year to school year. If we teach students the most important skills, they will be able to unlock any content.

It is the skills that help students learn content.

The truth about teaching is that we need students to learn quite a bit of content on their own (through homework, peer work or independent work in class). In truth, our direct teaching time is so limited that the only way they will master all of the content is if we give them the skills to learn with us and also on their own.

EXAMPLE

For example, as a teacher of history I might think…

Cramming the most content in by a certain date on the calendar is a really common way of thinking. Trust me… I am very familiar with this. I kept going with this approach even when I had proof in my students' test scores that it wasn't working. I am a slow learner, obviously!

But what if that same history teacher thought like this:

You can see these three things at play in this example:

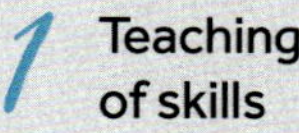
1 Teaching of skills

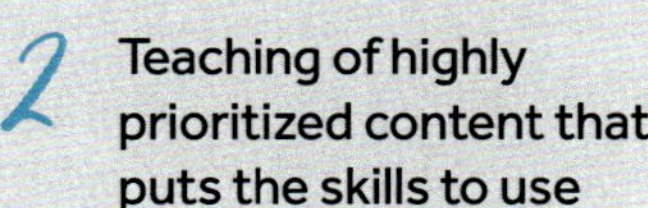
2 Teaching of highly prioritized content that puts the skills to use

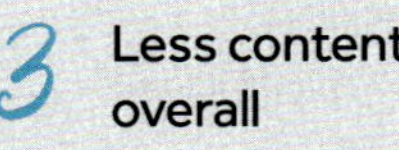
3 Less content overall

Uncluttered instruction gives more time to focus, to make connections and let it all sink in!

Even though we have become nearly obsessed with "getting through the content," directly teaching skills is the **NAME** *of the* **GAME.**

The
1-SHEET

The first simplifying tool I am going to recommend that you use is the 1-sheet. It will be the main tool we'll use to plan our lessons every day.

The 1-sheet is designed to do two things for you as you lesson plan:

 Put the most important skills/content in a tidy little container so that you stay focused

 Put up healthy boundaries so that you don't overplan

---

REALITY CHECK:

It's called a 1-sheet for a reason. It is ONE SHEET. Font size 11 or 12. Not 8 sheets or a 1-sheet in font size 3. Yep…I know all the tricks!

On the facing page, you'll see your first example of a 1-sheet! It is the overview of what you'll learn throughout this book.

I actually followed my own advice and completed the 1-sheet first and then wrote this entire book from it…that is how helpful and simple it is!

Later in the book, I will teach you how to fill in your own 1-sheet as you lesson plan. Also, your students can use it, too!

THE ACTUAL 1-SHEET I USED TO WRITE THIS BOOK

Get Real and Cut Down

In order for students to master your content, you will have to considerably pare down how much you are teaching.

Don't Let the Language Get You!

Let's get a baseline understanding on the terms we hear and use often around the topic of lesson planning:

- **Standard:** What to teach and what should be mastered at the end of the school year
- **Goal:** General statement on the purpose of the lesson (oftentimes uses interchangeably with 'standard')
- **Objective:** The skill I want the students to learn
- **Outcome:** How students will demonstrate the skill to show mastery

Pre-Plan the Failures

Plan for and teach through tripping points in your lesson. Common tripping points might be: not enough background information, inability to take notes, lack of retention from one lesson to another or dense vocabulary.

Skills Over Activities

Even though we have become nearly obsessed with "getting through the content," directly teaching skills is the name of game. For example, if students don't know how to analyze a piece of text (*a skill*), then they will not be able to determine the differences and similarities between Shakespeare's first and second major works (*content*).

Build in Accountability

This means that every student is doing something related to the content at all times. There are really only three ways we know our students are doing the work: they are writing something, saying something or giving some sort of physical response.

Put it in Logical Order

- **Months 1-3:** Which standards need to be taught as a foundation for other standards to come?
- **Months 4-6:** Which standards have logical connections to the standards that they have already mastered?
- **Months 7-9:** Which standards require students to apply all that they have learned with more complex content?

Take it Apart

What does this standard assume my students already know or need to know how to do?

Two things are happening when you ask and answer that question:

1. You are unearthing the hidden assumptions in the standard
2. You are focusing on the teachable and learnable skills within each standard

Choose the Stuff that Matters

Ask yourself: What is the vital 20% of skill/content that is actually producing the mastery that I need my students to have?

A Crash Course in Lesson Planning

THE BIG 5 OF LESSON PLANNING

BIG IDEA 1

A lesson plan is your detailed roadmap of:

1. What will be taught
2. How it will be taught
3. How it might be modified for particular students or in response to feedback
4. How you and your students will know they have mastered the content

BIG IDEA 2

There is a difference between lesson planning and lesson prepping.

▸ **Lesson planning** is the detailed roadmap of WHAT you'll teach (content, curriculum, skill, etc.).

▸ **Lesson prepping** is the detailed roadmap of HOW it will be delivered to the students (engagement techniques, written/verbal/physical responses, small group/whole group, etc.).

The Simplified Lesson Planning Formula will always incorporate both lesson planning and lesson prepping!

THE BIG 5 OF LESSON PLANNING

BIG IDEA 

There is also a big difference between teaching a skill and teaching an activity.

▶ **A skill** is the ability to do something with expertise.

Skill examples: Being able to determine the initial sound in a word, writing a brief summary of a piece of text or discussing the pros and cons of a topic.

▶ **An activity** is an opportunity to practice or apply a known skill.

Activity examples: Playing a picture sort game that requires students to sort picture cards by initial sounds, partnering up for a reading skills game or completing a graphic organizer on the pros and cons of a topic.

This is an important distinction because we have to directly teach skills so that students can THEN go apply them in various activities. Putting activities before teaching skills often leads to content confusion and lack of mastery for students!

BIG IDEA 

In order for students to master your content, you will have to considerably pare down how much you are teaching. Simply put: **student mastery requires significant elimination and removal of content and activities.**

In fact, I think this is likely to be our biggest challenge as we work together to hone our lesson planning! We are going to have to train ourselves to realize that our students do not have to get absolutely every detail of our content to be prepared for the next grade level.

The Simplified Lesson Planning Formula will help you responsibly and thoughtfully pare down your content by answering four key questions:

1. What are the smallest chunks of skills/content that I need to teach and that my students need to master?

2. What is the vital 20% of skill/content that is actually producing the mastery that I need my students to have? And you did read that right: 20% of the skills and content! I promise you, it is not humanly possible to teach and learn it all!

3. In what order should I teach the chunks of content so that I increase the odds that my students will hit mastery?

4. What are the common mistakes that my students will make as they learn this?

THE BIG 5 OF LESSON PLANNING

BIG IDEA 5

The language around lesson planning has gotten way too fancy and confusing! So, let's simplify:

THE TERM	WHAT IT REALLY MEANS
"Standards-Based Learning"	When a teacher teaches skills and organizes instructional activities that help all students achieve the learning goals.
"Pedagogy" *or* "Content Related Pedagogy"	Matching the content you're teaching with the strategy or engagement technique that will increase the odds the students learn the content.
"Standards-Based Learning Activities"	The work that students engage in as they are mastering a specific, set learning goal.
"Instructional Sequence"	The steps you take to teach your students something new…also known as your lesson plan!
"Academic Language"	Words and terms that your students need to know in order to handle specific subjects. For example, in order to be successful in science, students would need to know and use words like "hypothesis" or "analysis" as it relates to scientific content.
"Assessment Criteria"	It is a statement that outlines how you will know if the student has mastered that lesson.
"Learning Target"	The skill you want the students to learn (same as objective).
"Relevance/ Rationale"	The reason(s) why the teacher chose particular techniques or strategies for use during a lesson. This is similar to pedagogy (see above).
"Formative Assessment"	The in-the-moment checks you use to see if the lesson is on target and to determine what adjustments might need to be made as you teach the rest of the lesson.

What is the **VITAL** 20% of skill and content that is actually producing the **MASTERY** that I need my students to have?

STEP 1: HOW TO LESSON PLAN YOUR SCHOOL YEAR

I hear the term "unpacking the standards" used quite a bit in schools. I know that some curriculum committees have even spent years taking grade level standards and breaking them into "sub-standards" and "anchor standards." To be really honest with you, I think this is a bunch of tomfoolery. Doesn't the standard already tell us what to teach?

It's busywork that keeps us treading water and never really translates into better teaching of ANYTHING in the classroom.

In an effort to get on with the teaching (which is the central idea of this book!), I want to lead you through a very simple formula for lesson planning so that you can:

1.   Identify what to teach so that students will master the standards

2.   Determine when you will teach it in the year, month/week and day

In my own teaching, I really only thought week by week and I realize now that the missing piece was knowing where I was headed month to month and semester to semester.

Knowing the big picture of where I am headed and how one skill builds upon another changes my teaching. It takes my students and me from, "What are we learning this week?" to "What are we learning this week that links to what we learned last week." This connection from week to week alone can be a huge game-changer!

So let's get started.

Throughout this book, I will refer to taking action at the beginning of the year, end of the year or in planning the whole school year. If you stumble on this book smack dab in the beginning or darn near the end of the year, IT'S NOT TOO LATE!

Start right where you are with the time you have left in the school year. Nothing I encourage you to do is so precious that you have to have perfect timing. And, by the way, there is no such thing as "perfect timing" in education so let's not use it as an excuse for not starting RIGHT NOW!

DECONSTRUCT WHAT YOU'LL TEACH

First, we are going to deconstruct what you have to teach. When you deconstruct something, you take it apart in order to expose its hidden internal assumptions. This is exactly what is missing from typical lesson planning.

We try to hammer away at teaching a standard over and over until they "get it." We fail to realize that they don't get it because we haven't exposed the hidden internal assumptions for that standard.

In other words, we haven't taught the skills underpinning the mastery of that standard.

For example, let's say that this year I have to teach my 5th graders how to "Compare and Contrast the overall structure (e.g., chronology, comparison, cause/effect, problem/solution) of events, ideas, concepts, or information in two or more texts." That is just one of the end-of-year standards expectations for my students!

The problem is, that standard doesn't tell me all of the underpinning skills that have to be mastered in order for my students to hit that end-of-year goal. If I don't teach those skills, many of my students won't master that standard at the end of the year.

So this is where your year-long lesson plan comes in.

Materials:

- ☐ Copy of the standards for your grade level or courses you teach

- ☐ Large chart paper

- ☐ Chart paper markers

- ☐ Printed copy of a free online academic calendar for this school year with one month per page (and boxes big enough to write in) for EACH of the subjects or courses you teach

- ☐ Copy of your district's curriculum map or program scope and sequence, if you are required to lesson plan using them

Activity

On each ½ page of chart paper, write the standard that you have to teach (so that you have two standards per piece of chart paper). If your standards are in a particular order, list them on the chart paper in order.

EXAMPLE

> Compare and contrast the overall structure (e.g., chronology, comparison, cause/effect, problem/solution) of events, ideas, concepts, or information in two or more texts.

> Analyze multiple accounts of the same event or topic, noting important similarities and differences in the point of view they represent.

If you teach quarter or semester classes only or do not have your students for the entire school year, you can adjust this part and plan for the semester or quarter instead of the whole school year. Super simple adjustment!

Now you're going to ask yourself this question as you work standard-by-standard: "What does this standard assume my students already know how to do?" Then, write those skills down beneath the standard on the chart paper.

Two things are happening when you ask and answer that question:

1. You are unearthing the hidden assumptions in the standard (remember our definition of "deconstruct?")

2. You are focusing on the teachable and learnable skills within each standard which are essential for mastery

So, this is what it would look like for me to add the underpinning skills to the example on the previous page:

Compare and contrast the overall structure (e.g., chronology, comparison, cause/effect, problem/solution) of events, ideas, concepts, or information in two or more texts.

– Compare
– Contrast
– Know the five types of informational text structures
– Know the purposes and uses behind the five types of text structures
– Apply the five types of text structures to two texts and compare/contrast

Analyze multiple accounts of the same event or topic, noting important similarities and differences in the point of view they represent.

– Set up notes to analyze multiple sources
– Determine what the "important" similarities are
– Determine what the "important" differences are
– Steps for text analysis

I want to make sure that you don't lose your mind with the task and end up with 492 things to teach beneath every single standard. I stick to the top 4-5 underpinning skills for each and then move on. Repeat after me, "I will not overthink this. I will not overthink this." That is our mantra for this step.

Now, go through your standards and add your 4-5 underpinning skills for each on the chart paper. I usually give myself (or my team, if we are working together on this) 3 minutes per standard. That's it!

The really great news? You will only need to do this one time unless you change grade levels or departments!

ORDER THE SKILLS

Whew! You've done the heavy lifting and this next part will be simple.

You're now going to go back to the underpinning skills lists for each of your standards and you're going to ask yourself: "What is the most logical order in which to teach these underpinning skills?"

What we're doing here is creating logical building blocks of skills as we inch closer and closer to mastering that end-of-year standard. The order of these skills has to make sense to you so that your lesson planning and instruction will be connected and as easy to teach as possible.

Compare and contrast the overall structure (e.g., chronology, comparison, cause/effect, problem/solution) of events, ideas, concepts, or information in two or more texts.

1. Know the five types of informational text structures
2. Know the purposes and uses behind the five types of text structures
3. Compare
4. Contrast
5. Apply the five types of text structures to two texts and compare/contrast

Analyze multiple accounts of the same event or topic, noting important similarities and differences in the point of view they represent.

1. Determine what the "important" similarities are
2. Determine what the "important" differences are
3. Set up notes to analyze multiple sources
4. Steps for text analysis

Activity

Our old mantra is going to come back into play as you get to work on this step: "I will not overthink this. I will not overthink this." This step should take no more than 1-minute per standard because the order of the underpinning skills should be pretty logical. Go ahead and order the underpinning skills beneath each standard.

BUILD YOUR CALENDAR

This step is going to literally take you through planning everything you need to teach FOR THE ENTIRE SCHOOL YEAR. Yes...the entire school year. You may be thinking, "Well, I don't even know my students yet, so how can I plan the whole year?" or "I don't know what changes will need to be made, so it doesn't make sense for me to plan the entire year!"

Well, I am here with a friendly reminder that you MUST build your calendar for the whole school year or it's like you are flying the plane without using a flight plan. As a frequent flier, that doesn't make me feel confident at all!

You will create plans for differentiation and speeding up and slowing down your instruction as needed, but this is all about building your pathway from Day 1 to Day 180 of the school year. By building your pathway, you automatically increase the odds that more students will hit benchmark this year. I have seen it happen again and again with this simple plan.

Honest side note: I never did this when I was in the classroom. Instead, I started the year off and raced to the end and was usually disappointed when we hadn't hit mastery in all of the standards by Day 180 of school. Turns out my "race to the end" strategy wasn't a strategy at all.

Now here is where things get creative and you have a couple of different options! But first, let's determine which next step you'll take based upon which list best describes you.

Which list best describes you?

Teacher A

- ☐ You are required to follow a district's curriculum map or scripted program scope and sequence

- ☐ What you teach each month and week is laid out for you

- ☐ You can literally look at a calendar and see, "Oh! I need to teach students compare/contrast this week."

- ☐ In the case of a scripted program, the lessons for how you'll teach the standards are already written for you

- ☐ You use the district's curriculum map to know what to teach, but you are responsible for writing your own lessons that match the standard

Teacher B

- ☐ You create your own curriculum from the ground up

- ☐ You know which standards students need to master at the end of the year, but when you teach the standards and how you teach them is completely up to you

- ☐ You pick and choose resources from various books, websites, etc. to best teach each standard

So now we'll differentiate what you'll do next based upon your Teacher A or Teacher B status. If you are Teacher B, skip to page 21 for your next step.

Teacher A Directions

Pull out one of the calendar print-outs from Step 1 and get ready to write!

Choose one subject to start with. If you try to put all of your subjects on one calendar, it'll just get really jumbled. Working on one subject at a time keeps it clean and simple.

Now write on the printed calendar where you are going to teach each of the standards, according to your curriculum map or program scope and sequence.

If my school district's curriculum map tells me my students are tested on the standard "Compare and contrast the overall structure (e.g., chronology, comparison, cause/effect, problem/solution) of events, ideas, concepts, or information in two or more texts," on the 18th week of school, then I would go to my printed calendar and write that standard on the calendar six to eight weeks prior.

EXAMPLE

OCTOBER

Monday	Tuesday	Wednesday	Thursday	Friday
2	3	4	5	6
9	10	11	12	13
16 *Compare and contrast the overall structure (e.g., chronology, comparison, cause/effect, problem/solution) of events, ideas, concepts, or information in two or more texts*	17	18	19	20
23	24	25	26	27

Activity

Continue to do this for each of the standards your curriculum map or program scope and sequence has you teach until every standard is on your calendar. This will give you a big picture view of how much time you have to teach the standard. Time to move on to page 23!

Teacher B Directions

Pull out one of the calendar print-outs from Step 1 and get ready to write!

Choose one subject to start with. If you try to put all of your subjects on one calendar, it'll just get really jumbled. Working on one subject at a time keeps it clean and simple.

Next, you are going to make a logical plan of which standards you will teach first, second, third and so on. This can be really challenging because you might be thinking, "But wait! I can't delay teaching any of the standards... they all need to be taught right now!"

I completely understand this feeling, but we have to prioritize. Mastery is built minute-by-minute and we want to be able to engineer individual wins for students by giving them one standard at a time. A big key to this is not piling too much on your students.

Activity

Let's start to organize your standards and when you'll teach them. I like to make this step as simple as possible by asking myself these questions:

☐ Which standards need to be taught as a foundation for other standards to come? I place these standards as a priority to teach in months 1-3 of the school year.

☐ Which standards have logical connections to the standards that my students have already mastered? I place these standards as a priority to teach in months 4-6 of the school year.

☐ Which standards require students to use previously learned standards/skills and apply them in new ways? I place these standards as a priority to teach in months 7-9 of the school year.

Once you've figured out which standards you'll teach at the beginning, middle and end of the school year, it's time to place the standards on the calendar when you'll begin teaching them.

EXAMPLE

Let's say that you've decided that the standard, "Introduce the standard: Compare and contrast the overall structure (e.g., chronology, comparison, cause/effect, problem/solution) of events, ideas, concepts, or information in two or more texts," should be taught in month 3 of the school year, then you would place it on the calendar as seen below.

OCTOBER

Monday	Tuesday	Wednesday	Thursday	Friday
2	3	4	5	6
9	10	11	12	13
16 Compare and contrast the overall structure (e.g., chronology, comparison, cause/effect, problem/solution) of events, ideas, concepts, or information in two or more texts	17			20
23	24	25	26	27

Now, continue to do this for each of the standards you teach until every standard is on your calendar. Don't overthink this process and keep focused on what is just plain 'ol logical!

When you've gotten all of the standards on the calendar and you notice that one month is particularly heavy or light, feel free to shift them slightly.

What you have now is a total map of what standards you will teach throughout the whole year. This gives a big picture view of how much time you actually have to teach each of the standards.

STEP 2: HOW TO LESSON PLAN FOR EACH MONTH/WEEK

Now you are going to take the calendar and the list of underpinning skills that you created in Step 1 and focus in on the months and weeks. Again, your mantra is, "I will not overthink this! I will not overthink this!"

So let's get started.

The standard on the calendar tells you when you will **begin** teaching the underpinning skills for that standard. You are going to place the first underpinning skill on the calendar, starting on the date the standard first appears.

The next page will show you what this looks like.

I am taking my deconstructed standard with the underpinning skills and adding the skills to the calendar starting on October 16 (the day/week I said I would start teaching this standard in Step 1).

Monday	Tuesday			
2	3			
9	10			
16 Compare and contrast the overall structure (e.g., chronology, comparison, cause/effect, problem/solution) of events, ideas, concepts, or information in two or more texts — Know the five types of informational text structures + their purpose and use	17 Know the five types of informational text structures + their purpose and use	18 Know the five types of informational text structures + their purpose and use	19 Compare/Contrast	20 Compare/Contrast
23 Compare/Contrast	24 Apply the five types of text structures to two texts and compare/contrast	25 Apply the five types of text structures to two texts and compare/contrast	26 Apply the five types of text structures to two texts and compare/contrast	27 Apply the five types of text structures to two texts and compare/contrast

You may be wondering how long you should work on any individual underpinning skill or how many days it should appear on your calendar. I simply ask myself this one question:

"Is this a brand-new skill or is this a skill I am building on from a previous grade level?"

If I am teaching the underpinning skill for the first time (which is actually pretty rare, considering how most standards build from one grade level to the next), I put that underpinning skill on the calendar for 3-4 days. If it's not a new skill, I will put it on the calendar for 1-2 days. If I'm unsure, I'll put it on the calendar for 3 days just so I have allowed enough time.

You'll see this in detail on page 51.

PLAN THE MONTH/WEEK

Here is another example.

FEBRUARY

Monday	Tuesday	Wednesday	Thursday	Friday
		1 Analyze multiple accounts of the same event or topic, noting important similarities and differences in the point of view they represent. Determine what the "important" similarities are	**2** Determine what the "important" similarities are	**3** Determine what the "important" differences are
6 Determine what the "important" differences are	**7** Set up notes to analyze multiple sources	**8** Steps for text analysis	**9** Steps for text analysis	**10** Steps for text analysis
13	**14**	**15**	**16**	**17**

Analyze multiple accounts of the same event or topic, noting important similarities and differences in the point of view they represent.

1. Determine what the "important" similarities are
2. Determine what the "important" differences are
3. Set up notes to analyze multiple sources
4. Steps for text analysis

AVOID THE FREAK OUT!

You might feel overwhelmed with all that you have to teach when you look at your year this way. This is totally normal! Once we break down the daily lesson formula in the next section of the book, everything will start to fall into place.

You will likely overlap your work on some standards because they fit together, have the same underpinning skills or make sense to teach at the same time. You are probably already seeing evidence of this.

If you are a teacher working from a curriculum map or program scope and sequence, this step is just about filling in your curriculum map and getting down to the lesson level. When I was teaching from a curriculum map, even though the standards or goals were laid out for me, I still had to do a TON of lesson planning to get my students there! That is what this step is all about.

If you see a couple of standards or underpinning skills on one day that don't seem to connect or make sense together...DON'T WORRY! Step 3 of our formula is going to help you link everything together very succinctly. Now is not the time for you to judge how you'll teach it...we will get there, I promise.

Big Alert! **Your students know more than you think!** I talk to so many teachers who approach their school year as if their students have had no prior teaching...and this is just not the case! They DO have skills and many times the simple teaching of the underpinning skill awakens previous knowledge which allows you to move faster through the plan that week than you had originally thought.

As you start to place things on the calendar, you'll fall into a rhythm with the underpinning skills and the pieces will start to fall into place. And as always, use your best judgment and default to what is logical and just makes sense. A lot of great teaching boils down to really practical decision-making anyway!

Activity

It's your turn now! Go into your Step 1 deconstructed standard charts and place on your calendar when you will teach each standard. Begin with the first standard on the calendar for the school year and place the underpinning skills for each of your standards on the calendar like the previous examples.

I will not
overthink this!

I will not
overthink this!

STEP 3: HOW TO LESSON PLAN FOR EACH DAY

Now it's time to take the calendar that shows what you should be teaching every day and put it into a very simple lesson form. This is where the 1-sheet will come back into play. It will be the main tool we'll use to plan our lessons every day.

I have created four different lesson planning 1-sheets that you will use based upon where you are in teaching specific skills and content.

The four Simplified Planning 1-Sheets are:

- **Teaching Something New 1-Sheet**
- **Practicing Something Known 1-Sheet**
- **Applying Something Familiar 1-Sheet**
- **Maintaining a Mastered Skill 1-Sheet**

Here's how you will determine which one you will use:

If you are teaching a skill/content that is brand-new which students have not been directly taught before

Then use  → 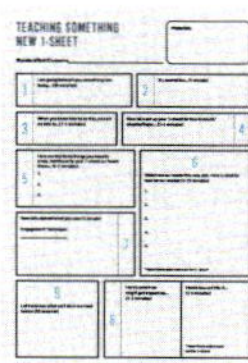

Teaching Something New 1-Sheet

If you are following-up on something which you've taught or which was taught in a previous class or grade level

Then use  → 

Practicing Something Known 1-Sheet

If students are ready to combine skill/content with other skill/content they have previously learned

Then use → 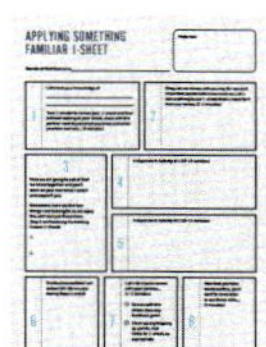

Applying Something Familiar 1-Sheet

If students are in need of a little skill touch-up because it has been a while since it was taught

Then use → 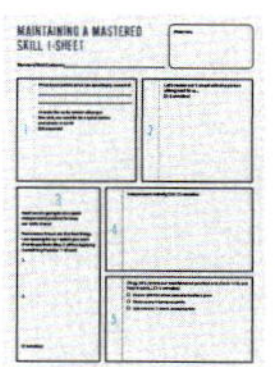

Maintaining a Mastered Skill 1-Sheet

Important Note: As you get comfortable with the different 1-sheets, you will notice that they are built upon the explicit lesson format:

- **Teach:** Directly telling the students what they need to know
- **Model:** Showing them what it looks like when they are doing the thing you are teaching them
- **Guided Practice:** Practicing the skill as a whole class through a structured activity
- **Application:** Taking the new thing they've learned and applying it independently
- **Maintenance:** Checking in on the skill and practicing it to ensure long term mastery

You are automatically taking your students through the explicit lesson planning steps by using the four 1-sheets because it is built right into them! One less thing for you to worry about!

You will also notice that the Simplified Lesson Planning 1-sheets help control instructional clutter.

Here are some examples of instructional clutter that interfere with mastery of key skills:

- Too much background information that preempts what will be taught in the lesson

- Changing routines and procedures too often in an effort to keep things fresh and new

- Turning instruction into a game or activity in an effort to keep students interested

- Using too many graphic organizers or anchor charts to explain or reinforce concepts

- Introducing more vocabulary words and word lists than students could ever master

- Using engagement techniques that are too intricate and implemented so often that they become the focus

Trust me on this: students are highly engaged in lessons when they experience great success. **Increasing the odds that they'll learn the content through simplification is your most powerful engagement technique.**

TEACHING SOMETHING NEW 1-SHEET

Materials:

Standard/Skill/Outcome____

1 I am going to teach you something new today... (30 seconds)

2 It's kind of like... (1 minute)

3 When you know how to do this, you will be able to...(1-2 minutes)

4 Now let's set up your 1-sheet for this skill/unit/chapter/topic... (1-2 minutes)

5 Here are the three things you need to know. Add these to your 1-sheet as I teach them... (5-7 minutes)

1.

2.

3.

6 Watch me as I model this new skill. Here is what to look for as I model: (5-15 minutes)

1.

2.

3.

4.

5.

*Have them add notes on the 1-sheet

7 Now let's debrief what you saw: (1 minute)

Engagement Technique:

____

9 Let's preview what we'll do in our next lesson (30 seconds)

8 Here's where we might get tripped up... (1-2 minutes)

Here's how we'll fix it... (2-5 minutes)

*Have them add a note on the 1-sheet

Understanding the
TEACHING SOMETHING NEW 1-SHEET

STEP 1

This is a simple statement of what you will teach and what they will learn.

EXAMPLE: *I am going to teach/review for you the five types of informational text structures today. Text structure is the organizational map that the author uses to organize his/her writing. You'll learn what they are and why they matter.*

STEP 2

Now you'll link the new skill to something that they already know about or know how to do.

EXAMPLE: *Knowing the five text structures and why an author uses them is like having a roadmap that will tell you exactly where you're going and what your stops will be along the way.*

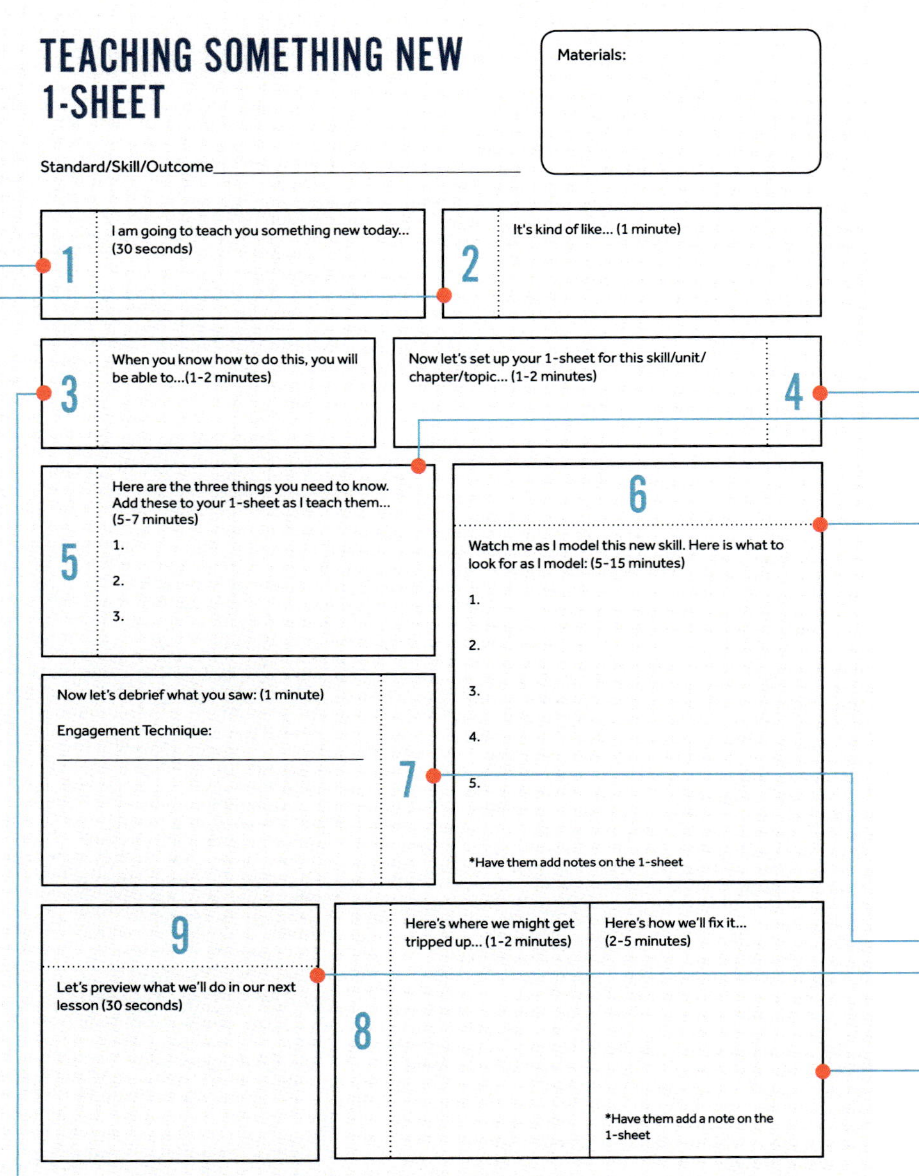

STEP 3

This gives the students the "why" behind the skill and grounds their work in reality.

EXAMPLE: *When you know the text structures, then you know where to go in the text to pick out the most important information.*

STEP 4

This is the step where you teach students how to set up a 1-sheet for the standard, skill, chapter or unit. Set up your own 1-sheet on the board and fill it out along with them.

Take a look on the next page to see how I would have the students set up their 1-sheet.

NOTE: If you are a primary teacher or a teacher working with students who are not yet writing on their own, then you should be keeping a 1-sheet for the whole class on the whiteboard or screen. The modeling of the 1-sheet should begin in kindergarten so that students understand the importance of notetaking.

STEP 5

This step gives the least amount of background information that you can get away with before launching into the lesson.

For this standard, I would teach them each of the five types of informational text structures, their purpose and use as well as clues as to the different types of structures. They would add these notes to the Five Types of Informational Text Structures chart on the 1-sheet as I teach.

STEP 6

The students watch as you show them what the skill from Step 1 looks like.

EXAMPLE: *Watch as I take the piece of text on pg. 281 in our history books and I determine what the text structure is by looking at some of the clues. Notice how I use the structure to find the most important information in the chapter. Here I go...*

STEP 7

Decide how you want students to reflect on what you demonstrated in Step 6 and choose a simple engagement technique that structures this for them.

EXAMPLE: *Okay, now that you've watched me model this for you, I want you to debrief with your small group using the Roundtable Share starting with person 2 and going clockwise.*

STEP 8

This step is all about cleaning up the mistakes before they even happen!

EXAMPLE: *Sometimes I've noticed that students try to apply text structures to narrative text. Actually these five text structures are only structures found in informational text. We use plot, character, setting, theme, etc. to decipher the structure of narrative text.*

STEP 9

This is a very brief peek at what will come next in the teaching and is designed to help students link one day's instruction to the next.

EXAMPLE: *Alright...tomorrow we're going to take what we've learned about the five types of text structures and practice identifying the text structures in a couple of new parts of our textbook. You are going to do really well at this!*

STUDENT 1-SHEET *example*

Standard: Compare and contrast the overall structure (e.g., chronology, comparison, cause/effect, problem/solution) of events, ideas, concepts, or information in two or more texts.

Five Types of Informational Text Structures

	WHAT IS IT	PURPOSE	USE	CLUES
Structure 1	Chronological			
Structure 2	Compare/Contrast			
Structure 3	Cause/Effect			
Structure 4	Problem/Solution			
Structure 5	Description			

When you <u>compare</u> two or more things you:

1.

2.

When you <u>contrast</u> two or more things you:

1.

2.

Steps to Compare and Contrast Two Different Text Structures:

Step 1:

Step 2:

Step 3:

Step 4:

Teaching Something New 1-Sheet *example*

TEACHING SOMETHING NEW 1-SHEET

Standard/Skill/Outcome *Compare & contrast overall structure in 2 or more texts*

Materials:
- *textbook*
- *notebook*
- *1-sheet*

1 I am going to teach you something new today... (30 seconds)
Know/purpose/use of 5 text structures

2 It's kind of like... (1 minute)
– *roadmap → stops*
→ where you're going

3 When you know how to do this, you will be able to...(1-2 minutes)
Pick out most important info

4 Now let's set up your 1-sheet for this skill/unit/chapter/topic... (1-2 minutes)
Table w/ 5 types, purpose, use, clues

5 Here are the three things you need to know. Add these to your 1-sheet as I teach them... (5-7 minutes)
1. *1. Chronological*
2. *2. compare/contrast*
   3. cause & effect
3. *4. problem/solution*
   5. description

6 Watch me as I model this new skill. Here is what to look for as I model: (5-15 minutes) *p 287*

1. *key words*

2. *repeating words*

3. *finding lists of things*

4. *checking to see if finding lists of things are in a certain order*

5.

*Have them add notes on the 1-sheet

7 Now let's debrief what you saw: (1 minute)

☐ Whole group technique for sharing:

____

☒ Small group technique for sharing:
Roundtable

☐ Partner group technique for sharing:

____

9 Let's preview what we'll do in our next lesson (30 seconds)

Take 5 structures and practice in 2 new parts of textbook

8 Here's where we might get tripped up... (1-2 minutes)

Here's how we'll fix it... (2-5 minutes)

Cause & Effect ——→ series of events
vs.
Problem/Solution ——→ starts w/ problem not an event

*Have them add a note on the 1-sheet

Increasing the odds that they'll learn the content through **SIMPLIFICATION** *is your most powerful* **ENGAGEMENT** *technique.*

PRACTICING SOMETHING KNOWN 1-SHEET

Materials:

Standard/Skill/Outcome_______________________________________

1
Yesterday we learned…
Let's review our 1-sheet and add 1-3 academic vocabulary words to the 1-sheet… (2 minutes)

1.

2.

3.

2
What questions can I answer for you?
(1 minute)

3
Today we are going to practice

____

a bunch of times together, using

____

for practice. I will be looking for you to:

1.

2.

(3 minutes)
*See #8

4
Here's how we'll group for practice together…
(1-2 minutes)

☐ Small group technique for working together:

____

☐ Partner group technique for working together:

____

☐ Individual
☐ Other:

____

5
Whole Group Practice #1 Activity
(10-15 minutes)

6
Whole Group Practice #2 Activity
(10-15 minutes)

7

Now let's review our practice…
(3-5 minutes)

☐ Review with the whole class any feedback given

☐ Add 2-3 academic vocabulary words to the 1-sheet

☐ Clean up any tripping up points

☐ Add notes to 1-sheet, as appropriate

8
Grades/scores/data I will collect during Steps 5 and 6
(20-30 minutes)

9
Let's preview what we'll do in our next lesson… (30 seconds)

Understanding the
PRACTICING SOMETHING KNOWN 1-SHEET

STEP 1

This step is a very quick review, focused on the 1-sheet. It grounds the students in what they already know, which is a huge confidence booster! If there are specific content-related vocabulary words you need students to master, you can add them to the 1-sheet now.

EXAMPLE: *Yesterday, we learned that authors organize their writing in a pretty logical way, making it easier for you to find the most important information. Two words that we learned as we read the text were: conglomerate and haphazardly. Let's add those important words to our 1-sheet now.*

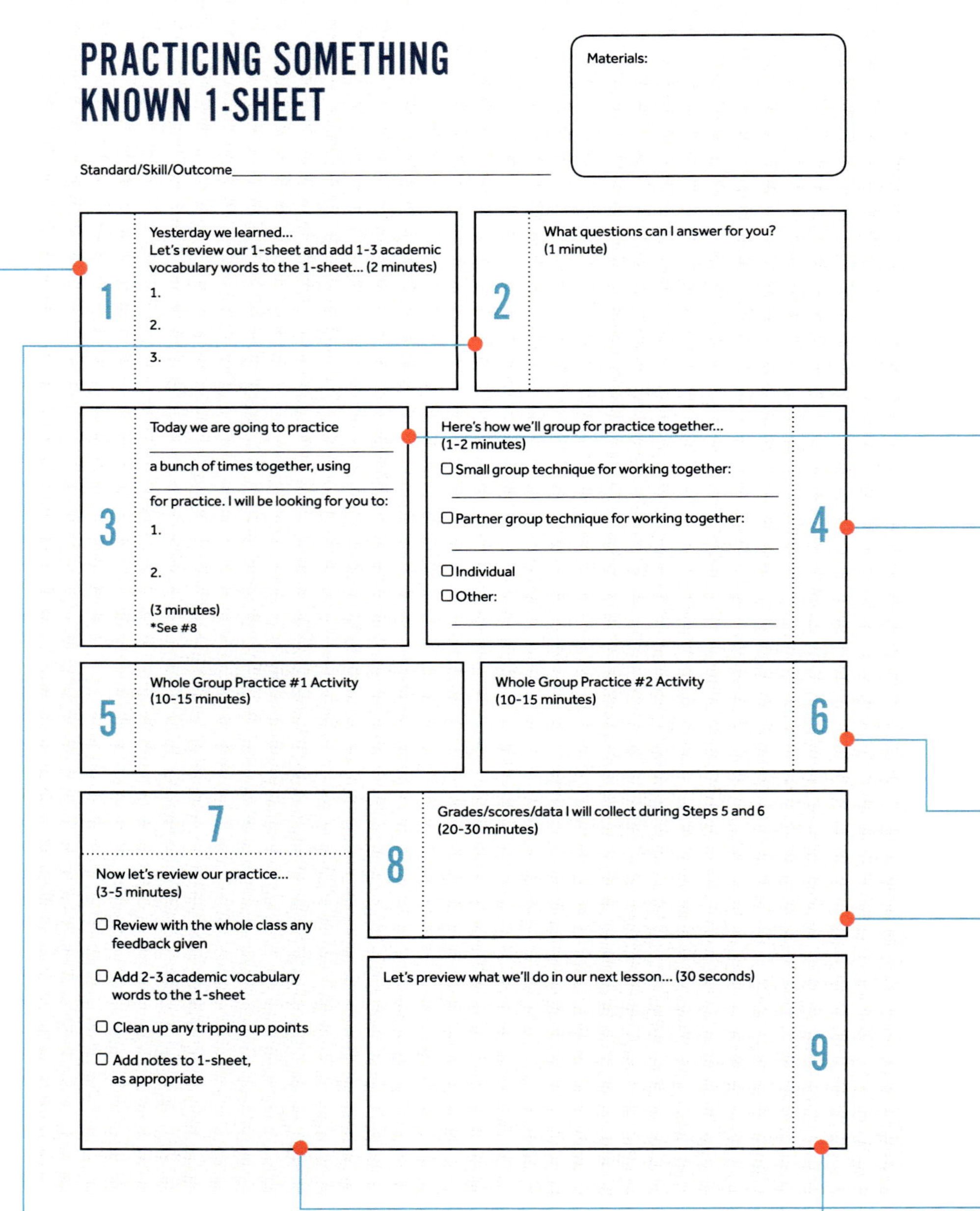

STEP 2

At this point, you'll do a check-in where students can asked for something to be cleared up. You might ask a student to quickly share what he/she learned the day prior or you might focus in specifically on a fix-up from the previous day.

STEP 3

This step gets students set-up for the task they'll do next. You will lay out for them what you will be looking for and what they will be graded on. This built-in accountability does two things:

1. Ensures that they start the task right away with purpose

2. Helps keep them focused on exactly the skill you're working on

Oftentimes, we over-explain things during our teaching. I hope you're noticing that we are highly structured, but quickly moving through these lessons. This is to give students time to do the work, not just listen to us talk about doing the work!

EXAMPLE: *Today, we are going to practice comparing and contrasting two different texts a bunch of times together, using pages 273-286 for practice. We will practice our skill of using text structure to compare and contrast while we're learning our content. It's really killing two birds with one stone! I will be looking for and scoring you on two things as I watch you work:*

1. *How you correctly identify the text structures in the text (you'll get 1-point for doing this correctly)*

2. *5-6 written statements from your comparing and contrasting of the two pieces of text (you'll get 1-point for doing this completely and correctly)*

STEP 4

This step is a simple set-up for how they'll do the activities together. Since this is a relatively new task, I will likely have them work with others during the whole group practice. The most critical thing to think about when determining what engagement structure you'll use is: What structure will best highlight the most important skills and content? The engagement structure is a tool for learning skills/content, not a whole activity unto itself!

STEP 5 & 6

Steps 5 and 6: See next page for details on these steps!

STEP 8

This step is just a reminder that you need to record the scores you collected during Steps 5 and 6! Notice that we aren't going to wait for some major project that is completed two weeks from now to give feedback and collect grades. Focused feedback each day leads to mastery and we don't want to delay it!

STEP 7

This step mirrors what you want students to do on their own each time they have completed a task: return to the 1-sheet and make any changes or additions. So, you're training them not only in skills and content, but in how to be an academic content master!

STEP 9

This is a very brief peek at what will be taught next and is designed to help students link one day's instruction to the next.

CHOOSING ACTIVITIES

One of the most important decisions you make during lesson planning is choosing what type of activity students will engage in to practice their newly learned skills.

The activity is the place where students practice the skill(s) you have taught and could take the form of filling out a graphic organizer, playing a game, designing a brochure, acting out a scene, conducting an interview, conducting an experiment, completing a task card or holding a discussion.

You will not struggle to find activities to fill in your 1-sheet, I promise! However, I want to give you some really specific guidelines for choosing the right activities for practice.

Whether you are purchasing resources from a site like Teachers Pay Teachers, downloading activities for free that were recommended via social media or are using a physical resource, I encourage you to use these questions to help determine if the activity is a good fit:

☐ Does the activity address the exact standard skill content that I am teaching?

☐ Does the title of the activity match what students will actually engage in during the activity?

☐ Does the activity introduce new content that is not related to what we are focusing on?

☐ Does the activity have my students practicing the standard/skill/content at the right grade level? Is it too simple or too difficult?

☐ Does the activity require me to do a big lead-in or can I quickly introduce it so that we can get right to the practice?

☐ Does the activity need to be modified to fit the Practicing Something Known 1-Sheet or can we use it as-is?

To be honest, I have used fewer and fewer online resources because I find that most are full of too much fluff! Oftentimes the title of the activity I find online might match the skill/content I am teaching but the activity ends up being too much "play" and not enough practice.

I find that I end up using simple activities like reading and discussing or filling out a simple chart more often than not.

You might be thinking, "But wait! I need to keep things fresh and exciting for my students!" And, I totally agree! However, I have found again and again that when students have success with a very simple activity, they are hooked and they want to do more of it!

Nothing builds engagement like success and confidence, so I encourage you to keep it simple and design activities where your students can be successful quickly.

Practicing Something Known 1-Sheet *example*

PRACTICING SOMETHING KNOWN 1-SHEET

Standard/Skill/Outcome _Compare & contrast overall structure in 2 or more texts_

Materials:
- textbook
- 1-sheet
- graphic org. on screen

1
Yesterday we learned...
Let's review our 1-sheet and add 1-3 academic vocabulary words to the 1-sheet... (2 minutes)
1. central idea
2. ~~2.~~
3. ~~3.~~

2
What questions can I answer for you?
(1 minute)

3
Today we are going to practice _compare & contrast_
a bunch of times together, using _p 273–286_
for practice. I will be looking for you to:
1. i.d. the structures
2. make 5-6 statements on compare & contrast of the 2 texts
(3 minutes)
*See #8

4
Here's how we'll group for practice together...
(1-2 minutes)
☐ Small group technique for working together:
____
☒ Partner group technique for working together:
Elbow partners during whole activity – both write
☐ Individual
☐ Other:
____

5
Whole Group Practice #1 Activity
(10-15 minutes)
compare & contrast graphic organizer for pgs. 273–280

6
Whole Group Practice #2 Activity
(10-15 minutes)
compare & contrast graphic organizer for pgs. 280–286

7
Now let's review our practice...
(3-5 minutes)
☒ Review with the whole class any feedback given
☒ Add 2-3 academic vocabulary words to the 1-sheet
☒ Clean up any tripping up points
☒ Add notes to 1-sheet, as appropriate

8
Grades/scores/data I will collect during Steps 5 and 6
(20-30 minutes)
1 pt – i.d. structures
1 pt – statements

9
Let's preview what we'll do in our next lesson... (30 seconds)
– pull all of our skills together to work independently using new text

Nothing builds
engagement like success
and confidence, so I
encourage you to KEEP
IT SIMPLE and design
activities where
your students can be
successful quickly.

APPLYING SOMETHING FAMILIAR 1-SHEET

Materials:

Standard/Skill/Outcome____

1

Let's test your knowledge of…

____

______________________________ .

Take 1 minute to review your 1-sheet and then without looking at your sheet, share with the partner next to you what you know and what you have learned… (5 minutes)

2

Okay, let me review with you any fix-ups and important points before we move on. Let's add anything to our 1-sheet that is important from our review. (2-3 minutes)

3

Now we are going to pull all that we know together and you'll work on your own while I watch and support you.

Remember, here are the two things I am looking for as we apply this skill (Pull these from Step 3 on Practicing Something Known 1-Sheet)

1.

2.

4

Independent Activity #1 (10-15 minutes)

5

Independent Activity #2 (10-15 minutes)

6

Grades/scores/data I will collect during Steps 5 and 6 (20-30 minutes)

7

Let's do a quick review with your partner… (1-2 minutes)

☐ Review with the whole class any feedback given

☐ Clean up any tripping up points. Add notes to 1-sheet, as appropriate

8

Now that you have mastered this, you'll want to remember to use these skills… (3 minutes)

Understanding the
APPLYING SOMETHING FAMILIAR 1-SHEET

STEP 1

This a quick and simple check-in on the 1-sheet. You'll notice that we tie the beginning and the end of each lesson to what they've learned and what they will learn next, using the 1-sheet as their guide. This repetition is on purpose and designed to build confidence and to remind them of how important the 1-sheet is to long term mastery.

STEP 2

At this point, you'll do a check-in where students can ask for something to be cleared up. You might ask a student to quickly share what he/she learned the day prior or you might focus in specifically on a fix-up from the previous day.

APPLYING SOMETHING FAMILIAR 1-SHEET

Materials:

Standard/Skill/Outcome_______________________

1 Let's test your knowledge of...

_______________________.

Take 1 minute to review your 1-sheet and then without looking at your sheet, share with the partner next to you what you know and what you have learned... (5 minutes)

2 Okay, let me review with you any fix-ups and important points before we move on. Let's add anything to our 1-sheet that is important from our review. (2-3 minutes)

3 Now we are going to pull all that we know together and you'll work on your own while I watch and support you.

Remember, here are the two things I am looking for as we apply this skill (Pull these from Step 3 on Practicing Something Known 1-Sheet)

1.

2.

4 Independent Activity #1 (10-15 minutes)

5 Independent Activity #2 (10-15 minutes)

6 Grades/scores/data I will collect during Steps 5 and 6 (20-30 minutes)

7 Let's do a quick review with your partner... (1-2 minutes)

☐ Review with the whole class any feedback given

☐ Clean up any tripping up points. Add notes to 1-sheet, as appropriate

8 Now that you have mastered this, you'll want to remember to use these skills... (3 minutes)

STEP 3

This step sets students up to work on their own and reminds them of the most important skills. Again, the repetition is built-in on purpose to boost student confidence and keep them focused!

STEPS 4 & 5

These two steps are exactly the same as Steps 5 and 6 from the previous 1-sheet except students will be working independently while you monitor. I will often use the same activity as I did on the Practicing Something Known 1-Sheet and will just ask different questions or use different text. Avoid getting too fancy at this step and use the guidelines on the Choosing Activities page to determine the best activities for independent practice.

STEP 6

This step is just a reminder that you need to record the scores you collected during Steps 4 and 5! Notice that we aren't going to wait for some major project that is completed two weeks from now to give feedback and collect grades. Focused feedback each day leads to mastery and we don't want to delay it!

STEP 7

This step mirrors what you want students to do on their own each time they have completed a task: return to the 1-sheet and make any changes or additions. So, you're training them not only in skills and content, but in how to be an academic content master!

STEP 8

Oftentimes it may look like students have forgotten how to do a skill you have previously taught, but in reality they have just forgotten to use it. This step ensures that they will keep the skill/content fresh by using it regularly.

Note on the 1-Sheet

I have students keep a binder of the 1-sheets as we complete them. So at this point, I have them add the 1-sheet for this skill to a tab in their binder so they can refer to it regularly and also have it on hand for the skill maintenance work that we'll do in the next 1-3 months!

PLAN FOR EACH DAY

Applying Something Familiar 1-Sheet *example*

APPLYING SOMETHING FAMILIAR 1-SHEET

Standard/Skill/Outcome _Compare & contrast overall structure in 2 texts_

Materials:
– 1-sheet
– textbook

1
Let's test your knowledge of...
Compare & contrast overall structure in 2 texts .

Take 1 minute to review your 1-sheet and then without looking at your sheet, share with the partner next to you what you know and what you have learned... (5 minutes)

(brand new partner)

2
Okay, let me review with you any fix-ups and important points before we move on. Let's add anything to our 1-sheet that is important from our review. (2-3 minutes)

Reminder: the reason we do this is because the structure of text tells us where the most important info is found in the text = CONTENT

3
Now we are going to pull all that we know together and you'll work on your own while I watch and support you.

Remember, here are the two things I am looking for as we apply this skill (Pull these from Step 3 on Practicing Something Known 1-Sheet)

1. _i.d. the structures_

2. _use the structures to find most important content_

4
Independent Activity #1 (10-15 minutes)

Go back to Chap 2 in textbook and use the skill to answer this:
Now that you know how to use text structure, what more info did you learn about Chap 2's content?

5
Independent Activity #2 (10-15 minutes)

Brand new text (first read): Chapter 6 p299-311 (2 texts)
–Read
–i.d. text structure
–compare & contrast
–answer chapter questions on p312

6
Grades/scores/data I will collect during Steps 5 and 6 (20-30 minutes)

1. i.d. text structure in steps (1 pt.)

2. Compare & contrast (7 pt.)

3. p312 questions (grade together... up to 10 pts)

7
Let's do a quick review with your partner... (1-2 minutes)

☒ Review with the whole class any feedback given

☒ Clean up any tripping up points. Add notes to 1-sheet, as appropriate

8
Now that you have mastered this, you'll want to remember to use these skills... (3 minutes)

–any time you have a first read on informational text

It is one thing to **GET** your students to mastery. It's a whole other thing to **KEEP** them there!

MAINTAINING A MASTERED SKILL 1-SHEET

Materials:

Standard/Skill/Outcome____

1
It has been awhile since we specifically looked at

____

____.

In order for us to remain strong in this skill, we need to do a quick review and check-in on it!
(30 seconds)

2
Let's review our 1-sheet with the person sitting next to us...
(2-3 minutes)

3

Next we are going to do a quick independent practice to keep our skills sharp!

Remember, these are the two things I am looking for as I watch you work (Pull these from Step 3 of the Applying Something Familiar 1-Sheet)

1.

2.

(2 minutes)

4
Independent Activity (10-15 minutes)

5
Okay, let's review our maintenance practice and check-in to see how it went... (1-2 minutes)

☐ Review with the whole class any feedback given

☐ Clean up any tripping up points

☐ Add notes to 1-sheet, as appropriate

PLAN FOR EACH DAY

Understanding the
MAINTAINING A MASTERED SKILL 1-SHEET

STEP 1

This step is a very simple connection back to the skill you have already taught and they have already practiced.

STEP 2

This step is a very simple connection back to the 1-sheet and gives students an opportunity to refresh their memory and quiz each other a bit!

STEP 3

This step sets students up to work on their own and reminds them of the most important skills. Again, the repetition is built-in on purpose to build student confidence and keep them focused!

STEP 4

Refer to the Choosing Activities page to determine the best activity for independent practice.

STEP 5

By this time, you have set the routine that students will always return to their 1-sheet, add anything new, clean up any tripping points and review feedback. You will have also taught other skills in the meantime which you can link to this skill.

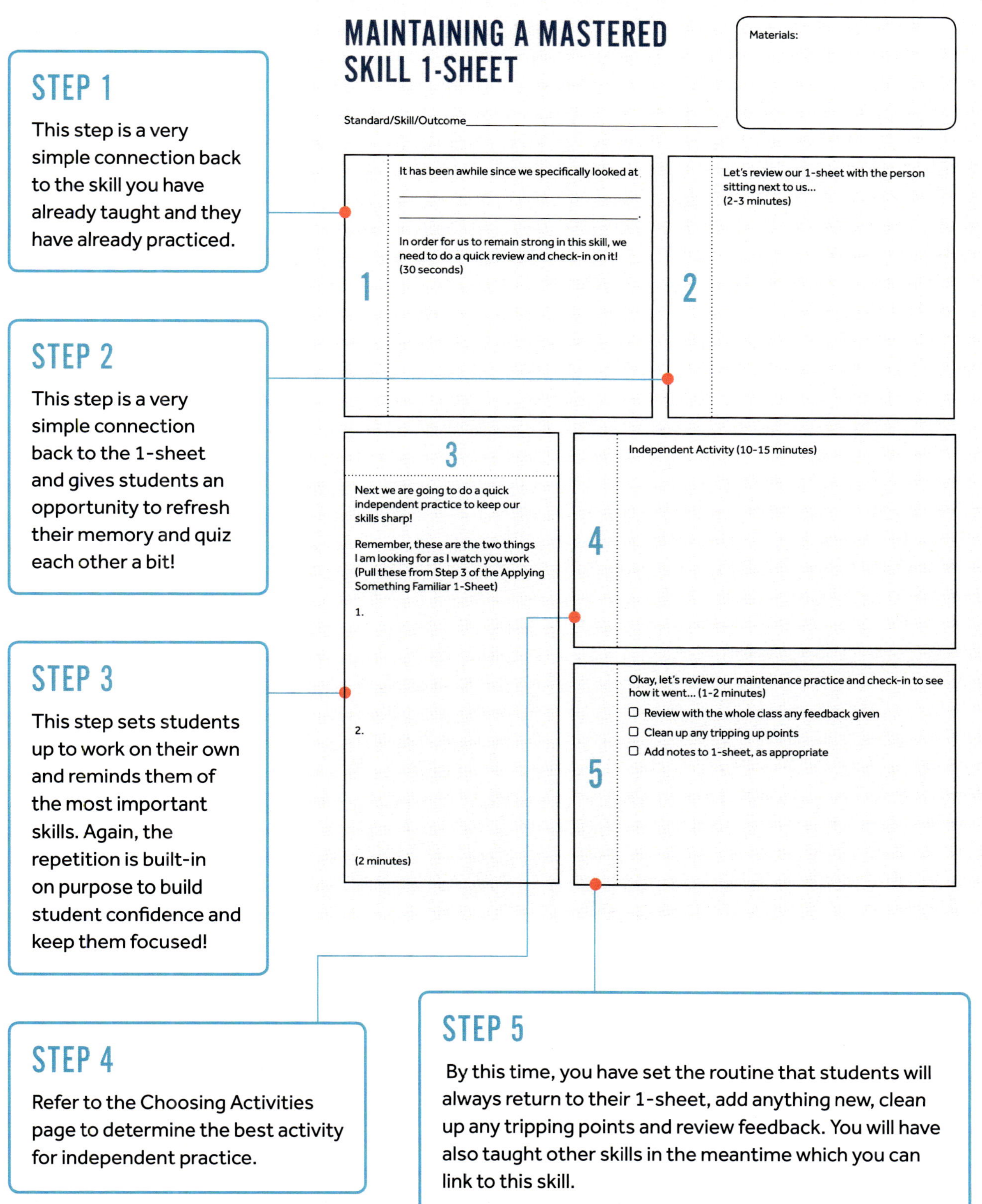

Maintaining a Mastered Skill 1-Sheet *example*

MAINTAINING A MASTERED SKILL 1-SHEET

Standard/Skill/Outcome _Compare & contrast structure in 2 or more texts_

Materials:
- 1-sheet for this skill
- textbook

1

It has been awhile since we specifically looked at _how to use text structure to find the most important info_ .

In order for us to remain strong in this skill, we need to do a quick review and check-in on it! (30 seconds)

2

Let's review our 1-sheet with the person sitting next to us... (2-3 minutes)

-elbow partner share (have 1 partner share something that stood out)

3

Next we are going to do a quick independent practice to keep our skills sharp!

Remember, these are the two things I am looking for as I watch you work (Pull these from Step 3 of the Applying Something Familiar 1-Sheet)

1. _i.d. text structure_

2. _use structure & find most important info._

(2 minutes)

4

Independent Activity (10-15 minutes)

Use compare & contrast text structures graphic org. w/ current text on p333–339

5

Okay, let's review our maintenance practice and check-in to see how it went... (1-2 minutes)

☒ Review with the whole class any feedback given

☒ Clean up any tripping up points

☒ Add notes to 1-sheet, as appropriate

link to how they use text structure in their own writing

3, 4, AND 5 DAY PLANS FOR USING THE 1-SHEETS

If your yearly calendar has you teaching a new underpinning skill for **3 DAYS**, it might look like this:

Day 1 of New Underpinning Skill	Day 2 of New Underpinning Skill	Day 3 of New Underpinning Skill	1-2 Months Out
Use	*Use*	*Use*	*Use*
Teaching Something New 1-Sheet	Practicing Something Known 1-Sheet	Applying Something Familiar 1-Sheet	Maintaining a Mastered Skill 1-Sheet

If your yearly calendar has you teaching a new underpinning skill for **4 DAYS**, it might look like this:

Day 1 of New Underpinning Skill	Day 2 of New Underpinning Skill	Day 3 of New Underpinning Skill	Day 4 of New Underpinning Skill	1-2 Months Out
Use	*Use*	*Use*	*Use*	*Use*
Teaching Something New 1-Sheet	Practicing Something Known 1-Sheet	Practicing Something Known 1-Sheet	Applying Something Familiar 1-Sheet	Maintaining a Mastered Skill 1-Sheet

If your yearly calendar has you teaching a new underpinning skill for **5 DAYS**, it might look like this:

Day 1 of New Underpinning Skill	Day 2 of New Underpinning Skill	Day 3 of New Underpinning Skill	Day 4 of New Underpinning Skill	Day 5 of New Underpinning Skill	1-2 Months Out
Use	*Use*	*Use*	*Use*	*Use*	*Use*
Teaching Something New 1-Sheet	Practicing Something Known 1-Sheet	Practicing Something Known 1-Sheet	Applying Something Familiar 1-Sheet	Applying Something Familiar 1-Sheet	Maintaining a Mastered Skill 1-Sheet

The above charts are not hard and fast rules for using the four 1-sheets. You will need to be responsive to your students and give them the teaching that they need most at that moment.

If they're really struggling with a skill as you're using the Practicing Something Known 1-Sheet, then use that one again the next day and just switch up the activities.

If they're really solid in the skill and are ready to move forward, then move quickly to the Applying Something Familiar 1-Sheet or Maintaining a Mastered Skill 1-Sheet.

Again...no overthinking, just logical decision-making!

So, let's say I am sitting down to lesson plan for the weeks of October 16th – 27th.

OCTOBER

Monday	Tuesday	Wednesday	Thursday	Friday
16 Introduce the standard: Compare and contrast the overall structure (e.g., chronology, comparison, cause/effect, problem/solution) of events, ideas, concepts, or information in two or more texts Know the five types of informational text structure + their purpose and use	**17** Know the five types of informational text structures + their purpose and use	**18** Know the five types of informational text structures + their purpose and use	**19** Compare/Contrast	**20** Compare/Contrast
23 Compare/Contrast	**24** Apply the five types of text structures to two texts and compare/contrast	**25** Apply the five types of text structures to two texts and compare/contrast	**26** Apply the five types of text structures to two texts and compare/contrast	**27** Apply the five types of text structures to two texts and compare/contrast

I am teaching the underpinning skill "Know the five types of informational text structures + their purpose and use" for three days that week. Here are the Simplified Lesson Planning 1-Sheets that I would use:

OCTOBER 16: Teaching Something New 1-Sheet
OCTOBER 17: Practicing Something Known 1-Sheet
OCTOBER 18: Applying Something Familiar 1-Sheet

I would then put this underpinning skill on a small sticky note and place it on the yearly calendar about 1-2 months out for maintenance practice, at which time I would use the Maintaining a Mastered Skill 1-Sheet to lesson plan.

The underpinning skills of comparing/contrasting October 19th, 20th and 23rd are pretty well known by this grade level, so we will just need to link their knowledge of comparing/contrasting to the text structures. I think I can go quickly through this one, so here are the Simplified Lesson Planning 1-Sheets that I would use:

OCTOBER 19: Teaching Something New 1-Sheet
OCTOBER 20: Practicing Something Known 1-Sheet
OCTOBER 23: Applying Something Familiar 1-Sheet

On October 24th- 27th we are going to do four days of pulling all of the underpinning skills together for this standard. Here are the 1-sheets I would use that week:

OCTOBER 24: Teaching Something New 1-Sheet
OCTOBER 25: Practicing Something Known 1-Sheet
OCTOBER 26: Practicing Something Known 1-Sheet
OCTOBER 27: Applying Something Familiar 1-Sheet

USING THE SIMPLIFIED LESSON PLANNING FORMULA WITH A SCRIPTED CURRICULUM

As I recounted at the beginning of this book, my lesson planning anxiety really ramped up when I was given a scripted program to teach. The irony of the whole thing was that our district adopted the new, scripted program to help us lesson plan!

The teacher's edition detailed what I should do, say and teach, so it seemed like the work was done for me already. But, I constantly wondered what I was supposed to put in my lesson plan book! I also had trouble figuring out how I could become confident with the lessons since I didn't write them and I knew for sure that I didn't want to just robotically read the script in front of my students.

What I needed was a study guide for my lesson planning! I needed a resource that would help me pick out the most important stuff to teach from the scripted lessons. After all, there was no way that I could teach everything in the teacher's edition with only 180 days of school.

If you are a teacher who is required to use a program where everything is laid out for you, then I would encourage you to use the 1-sheets to help you prioritize. You can use the 1-sheets as-is and just transfer the most important information over to the sheets (which is my preferred method). If you do this, you will have 1-sheets that will then tell you where to go into the scripted program and use what is there.

You might also choose to use the Simplified Lesson Planning Formula 1-Sheets as checklists or study guides for prepping each week. Let me show you what that might look like.

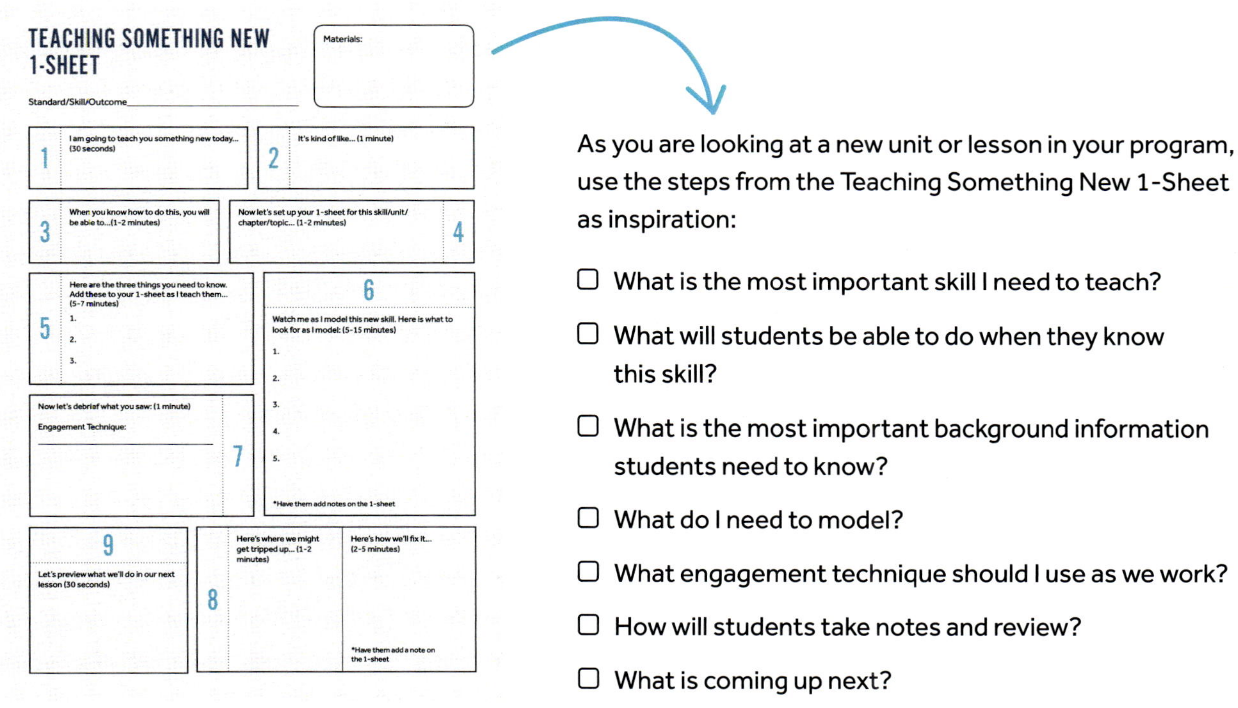

As you are looking at a new unit or lesson in your program, use the steps from the Teaching Something New 1-Sheet as inspiration:

- ☐ What is the most important skill I need to teach?
- ☐ What will students be able to do when they know this skill?
- ☐ What is the most important background information students need to know?
- ☐ What do I need to model?
- ☐ What engagement technique should I use as we work?
- ☐ How will students take notes and review?
- ☐ What is coming up next?

Once you find this information in your program, I would encourage you to highlight it within the teacher's manual so that you have a roadmap of the most important skill/content that you can follow during the lesson right there in the teacher's manual.

Reminder: This book is your **ROADMAP** for keeping what's important and replacing the rest with only what will serve your teaching and your students best.